Beacon Hunters

Beacon Hunters

signs of Light Along the Way

Field Notes by
Deb Grant
Lisa Hoelscher
Travis Meier

Jazzwater
Houston

Beacon Hunters
by Deb Grant, Lisa Hoelscher, Travis Meier

ISBN: 978-0-9824226-8-7
Jazzwater
jazzwater.com
Houston, Texas

Dedications

From Travis Meier
To my wife Kristen,
for your presence and patience.
You are a sparkplug for the imagination
and you help me to see the best in myself.

From Lisa Hoelscher
To my husband Danny,
and our beautiful girls, Lila and Josephine.
When y'all request a kitchen dance party,
I will always say, "yes."

From Deb Grant
To Garrett Sampson
You are a good man, Charlie Brown.

Table of Contents

Introductions by the Authors
Deb Grant

When I retired from parish and campus ministry, I took time to do nothing. As a friend advised, sometimes you just have to lie fallow. I enjoyed fallowing. Then, I began re-discovering my passions and my gifts.

I love writing. I had spent 37 years writing sermons. I wanted to play with other mediums such as poetry, essays, short narratives. So, I did. Next, I learned how to be a friend again without the assumptions that come with a pastoral identity. Still working at that. Friends are a never-ending joy. I truly enjoyed the students from my campus ministry days and cherish their friendship now. Travis and Lisa were two of those students now friends.

What I came to witness during our friendship was that we had a few things in common. One, we all became Lutheran pastors. Two, we all had an itchy interest in writing. Travis loved to express himself in poetry. Lisa hadn't found her favorite writing genre yet, but the emails I received from her were crafted things of beauty. Each of us had a voice, something to say and the time was right. I invited

9

Travis and Lisa to write whatever they wanted to write for this little book. It was a leap of faith for us. We didn't know what it would look like. The title and the theme of the book evolved when we saw our beacons of light running through the pieces. I am thrilled with both the process of putting this book together with my friends and colleagues and the outcome.

I don't believe gifts are given to be hidden. The proverbial light under a bushel is not a good place for light. Gifts are given for the sake of helping others. I am encouraged by the light in Travis and Lisa's writings. I hope, with the Spirit's help, you will receive the gifts this book has to offer so that they will spark the stories of beacons in your own life. +

Lisa Hoelscher

Back in college, I once ran out of quarters for the laundry machine in my dorm. Instead of making my way to the convenience store on the ground floor to buy gum with a five-dollar bill and get some change, I hauled my hamper to my campus pastor's house. She had taken pity on my low estate, and I, a broke college student, was thrilled. After a short time, I left her house with a stack of neatly folded laundry and made my way back to campus, patting myself on the back for saving four dollars. Sometime thereafter (it could have been hours or days, I've tried to block it from my memory now), I received a phone call from my dear, respectable, beloved campus pastor. "You forgot something." Oh? A textbook or my purse, perhaps?

No.

No, what I forgot was a pair of underwear. My underwear. I don't even know how it happened, but she was on the phone describing one pair of black underwear that definitely belonged to me. I could have died of embarrassment on the spot. Surprisingly, I didn't.

My campus pastor was clearly not shaken by a stray pair of undies, nor was she (on other occasions) shaken by theological quandaries, personal struggles, heart-felt confessions, or any number of life situations that we college students or other parishioners brought to her. She can handle dirty laundry, literally and figuratively.

And so, when she asked me to co-author a book with her and Travis, I did not hesitate to answer, "hell yes!" Even though I've never done this before, even though I had no idea what I would write. I trust her enough to take a chance. What follows is a smattering of thoughts, wonderings, inspirations, and a little dirty laundry. +

Travis Meier

I remember walking through the alley behind Martin Luther's church in Wittenberg, Germany and stumbling upon a pile of cobble stones. Having no idea how old they were or who was watching, I picked one up and thought, "Oh, the stories you could tell." Without a second thought I stuck it in my pocket and continued my late-night stroll. That weathered stone still sits on a shelf in my office, silently keeping its secrets, and staunchly providing inspiration. It indeed had stories to tell. Or rather, it had stories to help me bring to life.

Pastor Deb described this process to me in another way when I was a member of Aggie Lutherans during my time as a student at Texas A&M. She offered to me the art of finding sermon illustrations. Remembering moments and holding them in one's back pocket for later use. Keeping a weathered-eye on life unfolding for kingdom moments as they broke through in real time and in real space. Not just words on paper. But heartbeat and muscle and the living presence of God in our world. Stories to tell indeed.

Poetry has always been a part of my life. I have no idea where it started. Was it the lyrics of a song or a story at the edge of bedtime? No matter. Words and the patterns they could form have fascinated me beyond just the need to communicate the basic or mundane. Poetry and prose pull back the veil on the heartbeat of life. And every person has a story to tell and the words to use.

I was ecstatic when Deb invited me into this project. Having shared part of the road with both Deb and Lisa, sharing stories and God moments along the way, this is a great opportunity to share some of them with you. +

The Word Before the Words

by Deb Grant, Lisa Hoelscher and Travis Meier

In the ancient biblical story of Abram and Sarai, this elderly, childless couple of a nomadic desert tribe was given a promise, a vision in a dream that they would have home and family and be loved by their creator. In the darkness of their present situation, they found it hard to believe. They were told to go outside. They saw the desert night sky as it had always been, dark, foreboding, cold, filled with danger. The voice in the dream told them to look at the stars, count them if they could and consider it their future family album. That night, surrounded by all the same dangers as the previous nights, they saw what had been hidden by despair: beacons of light sparkling with a promise. That night they began a journey filled with obstacles and missteps, but nevertheless they began to move through the darkness with faith in the promise. We hazard to guess that they never looked at the night sky the same. In fact, we imagine in moments of despair, looking up at the stars in the night sky was an act of faith.

This story of darkness, wandering, and despair has repeated itself among God's beloveds throughout their journeys. It doesn't take much to know the troubles we've seen. It does take intentional energy to hunt for joy, to uncover what is hidden, to see what is right in front of us in a new way, to feel the illumination of wisdom. This is our time to be beacon hunters. Centuries after Abram and Sarai, there would come a prophet named John who bore witness to the light, to a teacher named Jesus whose followers were first called "People of the Way." Darkness and despair continue but so do signs of light along the way. The writer of the Gospel of John spoke of many signs and not all were written. There were many more signs. Perhaps the truth in the unwritten ones can still be found in lights along the way. Beacons of light can guide, reveal truth, teach, warn, inspire, encourage and shine on the faces of those who are on this journey with us.

This is the nature of faith. It is a journey without end, fluid, mysterious, dynamic. It runs and stumbles. It is the sound of one's own footsteps and the energy of a walking companion. It is a path blazing with sunlight or punctuated with penlights in shadows. All are generated by a power larger than us. Faith spans time. The journey of faith includes the authors of these field notes of poetry and prose. The journey includes you.

These field notes are raw observations that are personal but not private. They are intended to be shared. Truth when it is revealed is communal and allows us to look at what is before us in a new way. These notes may not resonate with yours. They may however evoke your own memories of light, your own discoveries along your way.

We wrote these down to make our joy complete in the sharing. We wrote these down to acknowledge the light of our own lives shines best when it is not hidden. We are all sparked with a divine light. We thrive on our journey when we see each other's lights. We are all beacon hunters. +

A Sentry of Light

by Deb Grant

I had my own newspaper route. I was nine years old. The newspaper bundled in wire was thrown from a truck onto my driveway. I cut the wires. I folded the papers in threes like a letter and stuffed them all into my canvas shoulder bag. My customers didn't want the paper tossed on their driveway or lawn. They each had a specific location. A side door. On a windowsill. Near a flowerpot. Under a doormat. Getting on and off a bike made the route feel longer and more tedious.

So, I walked.

The route spanned three tree-canopied avenues and one house at the midpoint that was built before the Revolutionary War. It was guarded by troops of lilies of the valley that always slowed my pace. They brandished a bold sweet fragrance with their tiny white bells.

Most days I finished the route and was home by sunset. I wanted to be home by sunset. I was young enough to still be afraid of the dark but old enough to be ashamed to admit it.

When the seasons and the time changed and the bundled delivery was delayed, it converged into a dark walk home. There were streetlights but not enough. The trees that formed a holy canopy during the day became looming giants that weaponized their shadows along my path. The pace of my step was a walk-run from one streetlight through the thick, colorless air to the next oasis of light where I lingered, slowed my breath, readied myself for the next sprint through my fear.

Many years later, I was in an airplane late at night. The plane was starting its descent for landing. From my window I could see small circles of streetlights. The little lights looked like pubescent soldiers standing at their post armed only with flashlights against an enemy camouflaged in shadows. Each sentry was surrounded. The darkness was truly overwhelming. From my vantage point, the light on their shoulders was barely able to create a circle the size of an umbrella. The sentries were outnumbered, yet brave and brilliant holding the miracle of fire against the advancing enemy of the night. My airplane window was still too high to see human movement, but I knew she was there. I knew there was at least one nine-year-old girl with an empty canvas newspaper bag running from sentry to sentry on her way home. +

A Thousand Pens

by Travis Meier

Some use brushes to communicate.
Others cast a vision
with hammer and chisel in hand,
striking stones
to leave their mark on history.
I've found ink
to wrestle with what
I want to say.
I've tried a thousand pens
in search of a conduit
between my heart and the page,
and a thousand times
I've found different markings
as I mimic the practice
of some well-worn sage.
Each instrument has a story to tell.
As does each human heart,
through which that vessel
it desires to impart
some thought or phrase,
to capture in amber
the echo of a life well-wrought. +

A Well-Worn Path

by Lisa Hoelscher

I don't much care for intense outdoor activities. If one day you need to find me and do not know my whereabouts, you can quickly eliminate any place where one would go camping, bungee jumping, rock climbing, mountain biking, skydiving, rafting, or spelunking. I will not be in those places.

However, I do enjoy a nice walk. A little fresh air, some greenery, a pretty view... that's what floats my boat, and I am particularly fond of a well-worn path. It just makes things easier. I don't have to guess where I am going. I don't have to wonder if someone else has already evaluated the path's safety. A well-worn path indicates that plenty of people have gone before me and determined that this path is a good one.

I like that. It reduces the work for my feet and my mind, and I can just enjoy my surroundings.

A psychology professor in college once told my class that neural pathways in the brain are like a well-worn path. The more you do a certain task, the more pronounced that neural pathway becomes. And every time you repeat that task, your brain has an easier time finding its way. With every repetition there are fewer obstacles. Ever arrived at home and thought, "wow, I don't even remember the drive?" That is a neural pathway at work. Your brain knew how to get home.

Even if it has been years since you've been home instead of just hours, your brain won't have to create a neural pathway from scratch. Just like a dirt path that has become overgrown, your brain can sweep back the long grass and discover the familiar trail underneath.

A well-worn neural pathway can be great when you're trying to find your way home, but well-worn paths exist beyond our brains or a field. Some well-worn paths are built into society and culture. Someone gets the ball rolling by taking a first step, then another follows, and soon a path emerges. But if no one speaks up to say, "could there be a different way?" *a* path could become *the* path.

I have heard of many paths that are the only path.

"We have always...
celebrated this holiday,
sung this song,
spoken this language,
pulled these strings,

made these jokes,
ignored those people,
attended this school.
We have always done things this way."

But as much as my feet and my mind appreciate a well-worn path, some paths aren't worth walking.

A few fellow walkers have already veered off in new directions across the societal landscape, unwilling to accept the well-worn path laid bare before them. The tools they pack vary but include determination, curiosity, hope, hunger for justice, longing for truth.

I know that a new path won't erase the old ones, even if they become unused and overgrown. I know that. Some of those old well-worn paths are practically permanent, and even tall grass will only camouflage what lies beneath.

But we can make new paths. All we need is someone to take a step in a new direction and invite others to follow. Soon, instead of bouncing back, the long grass will bend and break and a fresh trail will emerge. And one day, after enough walkers tame the tall grass, our feet and minds will rest on our well-worn path. +

The Choreography of Goodbye

by Deb Grant

Arrright, take care.

I didn't know how often I said it or how it
sounded until it was mimicked by a friend.
Arrright, take care...like a pirate.

Said, at first, to signal the so long
and then, ending with two serviceable words
with a touch of kindness.
Take care. You take care.
You take my care for you.
You take care of yourself.
Be careful in a dangerous world.
I want to see you again.

Personal salutations
with emphasis and inflection
that wear a unique pattern
on the soul like a shoe.
Repeated so often,
it comes to serve
as the ending punctuation
in combination with the movement

out the door, into the car,
hanging up, leaving the room.
The words and steps of the dance
become a comfort.

I knew a man who wore one-piece overalls
to church every Sunday.
On the way out the door,
he pumped my hand once and only once
from high to low and released saying
"Have a good week."

Until the Sunday he said, "Have a good life."

The one-word change in the lyrics of his dance
made me stumble. I lost my balance.
The rhythm of my step.
He was out the door.
I had to change my focus to the next in line,
to the next position
of hug or handshake or have a good day.

A few hours later, the overalls guy
sat in a chair in his living room
and shot himself in the heart.
His heart was weeks at war with grief
on the death of a wife of a lifetime.

Have a good life was still tenderly on his face
resting on his own shoulder away
from the violence done to his chest.

Since that morning at the church door.
Since that one-word change in his goodbye
I've been more attune
to the choreography of goodbyes.

Arrright, take care. +

A Race to The End

by Travis Meier

There once was a race to the end.
My Nana would pick me up from daycare
and we'd start chasing trains.
The call of the whistle
would send us scurrying across town
to the crossbars
and flashing red lights
in the hopes of catching
the elusive caboose.
Built to house the crew
who kept watch for signs of trouble,
the tiny, rocking shack
was the last in the line of cars
and the first in the line of defense
for the crew and cargo on board.
Now rusted and weathered
they linger like ghosts
in rail yards and museums
but their mystique still lives
in the memories of aging little boys.
Their lessons are not lost
with the growing wisdom that life brings.
We should always have an eye
for those we encounter.
The least and the last so to speak.

The ark could not close
until the Zebras had found their way inside,
or so the story goes.
A vision focused on the all
for the sake of the whole,
from the first last
to the last first.
The caboose was a sentinel
that housed watchful eyes
through long days
and dark nights
to make possible safe homecomings for all.
Our eyes and minds should be so faithful,
for neighbor and stranger alike. +

The Chapel

by Travis Meier

The wooden floor
creeks and groans,
desperate to tell its stories.
Of faded songs
and generation after generation,
the voices that echo
every time a guitar is strummed upon the stage.
Of chapel sleep outs
and teenage desires,
of sleeping cabin leaders
and daring moments.
Of fluttering hearts
and trembling lips
during the spark of a first kiss,
on the deck
underneath the heat of summer stars.
Of s'mores over a campfire,
as woodsmoke is spun
by the howling winds
of a cold-blue norther,
rattling through rusted window panes
during the Advent of a late November.
Of shaking hands,
as the words of a first sermon
are sent into the crowded throng

of friends and eager hearts.
Of silence,
as memories reel
and stories dance.
As the floating dust catches sunlight,
while the floorboards await
another moment
to be caught
and remembered. +

A High-Speed Funeral

by Lisa Hoelscher

Just yesterday I saw a car pulled over on the side of a country road. There was a house close by, but the car didn't belong to the house. The driver was crouched in the grassy ditch, and for a moment, I wondered if she was looking for something. But no, she was looking *at* something laying in the grass. A small, furry something with a collar. I couldn't identify it, but it was still.

Wherever animals and vehicles share roads, there will be animals who die by the wheel, windshield, or grill. It is part of the modern-day circle of life. It's unfortunate, but there you have it.

If you hit a butterfly, squirrel, or armadillo, you can probably go about your life with little to no trauma. Those animals belong in the wild and have no personal connections with people beyond passing glances and cursory interest. But when the animal is a small, furry something with a collar, it's different. You have killed someone's companion. Some of you may be able to keep driving and get over it, others (like me) feel pain, frustration, and remorse.

These murders are not premeditated, and they often occur quickly with no witnesses who could take the story back to the owner and explain the small, furry something's final moments. The little life just ends. No story is attached. Just, done. When the owner begins to wonder, "what happened to my small, furry something?" the question will go unanswered.

Unless the driver stops.

Not all drivers stop. Some don't want the hassle of finding the small, furry something's owner. Some don't want to confess what they've done. Some don't want to prolong their part of the story.

This driver - the one I saw on the side of the country road - stopped.

My eyes only saw her for a few seconds. She was on her haunches, looking at the nearby house. Then she looked down at the small, furry something with a collar, reached out her hand, and rubbed the length of it. I have no idea who she was, but I know she was kind. Her posture and shaky hand seemed to say, "I am here with you, and I am sorry, little one."

She was not alone in her sadness. I felt it, too, even as I drove past at 60 miles per hour. And she will never know this, but for a few seconds, we held a high-speed funeral together. I prayed for her and for the small, furry something's family and commended the small, furry something into the hands of the Creator.

This modern circle of life is unavoidable, I suppose, but I never want to be so indifferent to my power as a predator that I forget to stop the car and be human. +

Clarity

by Deb Grant

Second grade. I started flunking math. The math work process was to copy the problems from the chalkboard to our papers where we added the answers. The teacher would mark the wrong answers with a thick waxy red pencil that obliterated the numbers. We were required to make the corrections, but I couldn't read the numbers through the bloody response. My corrections were wrong, too. More layers of red. Try again and fail. I was frustrated and blamed the teacher for the carnage on the page.

It was a school nurse who alerted my parents that I might need to have my eyes checked. Sure enough. My eyesight was the problem. I was getting the answers wrong because I was copying the problems wrong from the board.

The day I walked out of the eye doctor's office with pink sequined glasses I saw what I had been missing. Three-quarters of the world's population needs corrective lenses to see clearly. I joined their ranks that day. The myopic spend a little time, sometimes a lot of time, on how we look in glasses or whether we should wear contacts. From that moment on, my glasses are the first thing I reach for in the morning and the last thing I let go of at night. I don't hear as well when I don't have them on. People who don't wear glasses think that is silly. People who wear glasses understand.

My father, who wore glasses himself, would sometimes call me to his side. In a quick move, he would lick his thumbs and smear my lenses with his spit. It would force me to take my glasses off and clean them. I always thought it was a prank. Most of the time it was. But maybe, just maybe, he was seeing what I chose not to see...that my glasses needed to be cleaned. I wasn't seeing clearly.

Now I figure out myself when they need a swipe of a cloth or a shirttail or a thorough rinse under a faucet. At some point, I start to be aware of a blur, a speck, a smudge, and I start to look at the mess instead of through it until I decide it is time to take them off and clean them. I settle them back onto my nose and the well-worn ridges of my ear cartilage. And that moment of walking out of the eye doctor's office happens again. I see what I have been missing. It's a little embarrassing but I get over it quickly.

I wish I could see without help but I can't. I've gone through glasses like old friends. Clarity doesn't just happen. It needs help. There isn't a day that goes by when I don't wonder what am I missing? There isn't a day that goes by when I don't spit on my thumbs and smudge my soul. +

A Reflection on Isaiah 35

by Travis Meier

A wasteland
of sand and time
to every horizon
my eyes could engage.
Parched tongue
weak knees
shaking hands.
Days unnumbered
and lost
to a faltering memory.
To surrender to death
maybe,
but the old promises
still linger.
"Say to those
whose sinew is failing
whose hearts are racing,
that the God of yesterday
today and
tomorrow
will come to restore
what is dehydrated,
forgotten and disillusioned."

Then suddenly
water.
The springs closed off
since the days
of the deluge
breathe forth
in an act
of creation.
Streams in the desert
dancing and singing
with abundance
and promise.
Roots long withered
burst into life,
shoots of green
breathing deep
the air of freedom
and release.
The lion and the lamb
gather by the oasis.
A flicker of Eden,
the spark of a forgotten dream.
And me
in my own mortality
remembers.
Bone to bone
sinew to flesh
the breath of life.
My lungs fill

for the first time
in a generation.
No longer a stranger,
depleted and lost,
but a child of the One
who has calmed
my racing heart. +

New Value

by Lisa Hoelscher

A couple years ago, I finally pinpointed one of my stress triggers. I was standing in line at an airport waiting to go through customs, and the wait was seemingly interminable. I tried to keep my cool; really, I did. But, I was soon shifting my weight from one foot to the other rather dramatically. I was emitting deep, audible sighs. It didn't help that I was pregnant, and my husband and I were travelling with our two and half year-old daughter.

As I looked upon the long line of people being served by just a few customs agents, my mind started working, solving all of the problems I could identify.

Obviously, they needed more customs agents in order to open more windows; an accelerated line for families with young children; better air conditioning to keep the stifling room cooler; clearer instructions on what we needed to fill out. And if they really cared about us weary travelers, they might even consider playing some music while we shuffled through the line.

Finally, I summed it all up and huffed out my assessment, "this process is so inefficient."

And there it was. The root of my stress in that moment and on so many other occasions: inefficiency.

The airport's customs process was (in my opinion) ugly and broken, because they hadn't optimized their workflow. And, surely, isn't that the point of life? To optimize your workflow?

I don't know where I learned that cold, corporate value. It wasn't ever stated explicitly like that in school or written in cross-stitch hanging on a wall at home (could you imagine a statement like "optimize your workflow" right next to "as for me and my house, we will serve the Lord?"). But it was implied everywhere.

"Make the best use of your time."

"Use your resources wisely."

"Do your best."

Only recently (and I mean very recently) have I realized that the pressure to pursue maximum efficiency is a sickness. We worship it like an idol, and we suffer the consequences when we don't worship it enough. Failure, thy name is inefficiency.

I see now its duplicitous attraction. Wanting an airport customs process to work well isn't a bad thing, but what happens when everything – and I mean every, single, blessed thing – in life is graded on its efficiency or optimal output? Suddenly, every daily task is judged like a high-stakes performance review. Did your morning routine meet, exceed, or fail to meet expectations? (Expectations, of course, being efficiency.) Did you eat three healthy meals, exercise, soak up the little moments, and let yourself be fully present for your spouse, children, family, friends, and co-workers?

It's absolutely impossible, and it's making me sick. Dare I say, it's making *us* sick.

Can we start valuing something else? Please?

Jesus was not known for planning his travel routes to reach the most amount of people in the least amount of time; meaning, he was not known for efficiency.

He would linger. He would wander. He would savor.

44

Can that be our new value, to savor? To savor is a blend of patience and gratitude and enjoyment that sets us free from ridiculous expectations and unattainable goals.

Think of the woman who anointed Jesus with expensive oil. THAT was not efficient. And when the disciples complained that the jar could have been sold for a ton of money, what did Jesus say? "Calm down, and savor this moment" (my translation).

He was just days away from the cross, but even that moment with the woman needed to be savored. Not beat into peak performance.

With our new value, to savor, perhaps now even waiting in long lines can be redeemed. +

Cristo Redentor

by Deb Grant

At the end of the day, I turn the steering wheel of
my car until it straightens on the driveway before
the closed garage door. I push the remote control
clipped to the sun visor. A deliberate motion. The
device sometimes slips off its clip and clatters to
the mat beneath my foot poised over pedals. If it
falls, I have to put the car in park and fumble on
the floor to find the opener. When I focus on each
movement, the remote stays in place and the
garage door lurches to open as if I had just woken
it from a nap.

I wait for the door to rise. Again, deliberately
because I can still see the dent I put in one of the
door panels because I didn't wait. Now I heed the
dent and wait until the door is well and good on the
ceiling tracks out of sight. I lift my foot off the brake
and nudge my ride into its stall.

I turn my head to the passenger side and wait until
the handle just above the passenger door window
lines up with the knot on wooden stud of the
unfinished walls of the garage. It is my way of

knowing that the car is pulled in far enough so that the garage door will clear and not so far forward that it will hit the wall.

I put the car in park, turn the ignition key to off, and just for a moment, my eye rests on the piles of boxes, a rake, a shovel, jars of nails and pieces of wood I can't seem to throw away. Horizontal studs of a pale pine two by four hold back tar paper and on one is a what looks to be a piece of dark green plastic, or resin.

I know what it is. It is a statue. No more than six inches high. A souvenir. A friend gave it to me when she returned from Rio de Janeiro years ago. High above the Brazilian city on a hill sits the 95-foot art deco statue of Christ the Redeemer. Cristo Redentor. Jesus with his hands outstretched. It is iconic. The celebrity of a million photos. Duplicated in souvenir shops on everything from tank tops to tiny green resin statues.

My tiny green Jesus had been packed and repacked and unpacked throughout my journeys. That time I was unpacking a box in the garage looking for something else. I lifted the statue out of the box and plopped it on the convenient stud. Green Jesus has been there ever since. Not on a mountain top but in my garage. Arms outstretched covered in some sawdust but still outstretched. Never any taller or shorter. And every day, it catches my attention after I put the car in park and turn off the ignition.

Sometimes that moment is altogether mundane. Not as utilitarian as aligning the handle of the passenger door with a spot on the wall to park the car just right. Sometimes that moment is altogether holy as if Christ himself had been sitting on the ledge of my garage all day to greet me. To welcome me home. To hold my face in his outstretched green resin arms just for a moment.

There is so much about the religion that seems impotent and as out of place in our age as a green resin Cristo Redentor in my garage. And yet. Mysteriously, green resin and a weary human collide into an unexpected greeting. To what ludicrous depths of humiliation will a Spirit stoop in pursuit of its beloved ones? Sometimes I sit still behind the steering wheel of my car in the garage and lean into the grace of the green Jesus embrace. There are chores to do inside the house. They can wait. +

I Hold in my Hand

by Travis Meier

I hold in my hand
a candle.
Bees made the wax.
God created the flame.
Prometheus opened the door.

Blue fades
to orange
fades to
transcendent.

The fire dances,
flickers and flabbergasts,
flirting with this mortal
in these minutes of prayer.

And I wonder,
does the candle change
or do I? +

On the Aftermath of Snow

by Travis Meier

The field was littered
with the creations of imagination.
The remnants of a great battle
in the cold.
The houses were still standing
and the trees chuckled in the breeze
at the events that had transpired.
Laughter rang out
instead of gunfire
snow balls flung
instead of bullets.

The joy of humans
coming together
in a brief window of magic
as snow had fallen
in a land that knew it rarely
and mostly through story and song.
Ah
the simplicity
of frozen water
and a lesson
on the best
of who we can be. +

The Day Jesus Sat on My Couch

by Lisa Hoelscher

For a while now, I have known that I want, that I need, to be close to Jesus. I have been feeling a bit disconnected from him. As if one of us were on vacation in a place with poor cell service and our calls (if we make them) keep going directly to voicemail. In reality, I have been a bit afraid of talking with him, because, well, it's Jesus. And you can't fool Jesus. There is no point in smooth talking, posturing, or putting on a happy face, because it just won't work.

I don't have anything super sinister that I want to avoid talking about, just your run of the mill doubts, questions, self-esteem issues, worries for my children... you know, the starter set of prayers.

And I'm sure my hesitation to talk with Jesus isn't unique. Plenty of people bristle at becoming vulnerable, at baring your soul to another. Even pastors. Even with Jesus.

But I need him. I want to talk to him in the flesh. No video call. No texting. No e-mail. I want to sit down in a place and know that if I reached out my hand, it would bump into his solid form.

I tried that the other day while sitting at my office desk. Kinda. I knew that I wanted, that I needed, to be close to Jesus for a while. And so I bowed my head in prayer, and I imagined Jesus sitting on the couch. Yes, he had a beard. Yes, he was wearing some robe-like clothing. Yes, he was probably whiter than reality. He smelled fine, though. Didn't say much. And as I sat safely behind my desk, the distance between us was great enough that I couldn't actually reach my hand out and check to see if he was really there.

But he was there. Oh, he was there.

That day, Jesus sat on my couch. And he listened. Jesus listened to my raw heart spill out my troubles, my worries, my questions, my hopes, my thanks. He respected my vulnerability and honesty. He created a space just for me. He didn't keep looking at his watch or eyeing the door. He would have sat there and talked with me all day.

It may have been my office, but I was his guest.

He disappeared shortly after our conversation ended, but the couch still held the weight of him, a sagging spot sunk into the cushion. As other people walk through my office now, I wonder if they can sense the change in the room. Maybe I'll put a

plaque on the wall, marking the day Jesus sat on
my couch. +

Holding Rope

by Deb Grant

Breakfast with a hummingbird
when over the shoulder of my house came
a beaded thread of larger birds.

Too high to recognize
except for their flying formation.
One in the lead then dropping back.
Never more than the lift of a wing away
from each other.
Their string constantly shifting but aligning,
tugging the line one way then another
as if they were nursery school children
holding a rope
to walk together through hallways or
to the playground.

I envied the birds' formation and
the children's holding rope.
Might we, at our more advanced age,
still need a holding rope?
Would we chafe at the idea of it?
Lose it? Drop it? Scoff at those still holding on?
Would we re-purpose the rope to suit our hate?

Could we find a holding rope that suits us all?
Can we agree to hold it?
We can always let go.
We are free to let go.
We know too well how to let go.
It is the holding that is hard.

What if we agree to be the holding rope?
What if there is something more than only me?
What if the more is we?
What if we choose not to let go
Even when we push and pull?
Until we all fly home? +

Mail Order Roses

by Travis Meier

My wife ordered a rose bush on the internet.
The picture showed beautiful lilac and blue
blossoms.
A new addition to our yard in the midst of an
unfolding spring.
I liked the idea,
but did not know what to expect.
When the box arrived
it was met with the usual excitement
that comes with the mini-Christmas
that shows up
with the mail carrier's parcels.
My pocket knife sliced through the tape
and the flaps opened to reveal
a horrible site.
Dry roots,
gnarled and cut
with stunted canes
stretching out, gasping for air.
The gnarled bush looked like a death mask,
the last-breath cast of a life gone,
something you'd find in a flower bed
after a long winter
and cast to the curb without a second thought.
Any yet,

this collection of stems and cells
was meant to be planted.
It promised renewal, blossoms, and buds.
So later I'll take my shovel
and get to work
turning soil and making a new home
for this parched and petrified traveler.
Soon roots will take hold,
life will continue,
flowers will bloom,
and rose petals will fall
gracefully in the breeze.
Such is the promise of life and Lent.
The deserts will be traversed
and water will find parched places.
New beginnings will take root
in the darkness before first light and a new day.
Ultimately death's tomb contains only
a folded shroud,
and scarred hands will show us resurrection.
Life ebbs and flows,
contains stretches of growth and fallow fields
in their due season.
And like the dehydrated rose bush
in a box in my living room,
we will find that the gardener has already been
hard at work
with shovel in hand,
preparing a place for us

to stretch our roots
and grow. +

The Game

by Lisa Hoelscher

They say that scent is the strongest sense tied to memory, and I believe that they are correct. "They" being that amorphous group of experts which people call upon to support all kinds of personal opinions and decisions. In this case though, I feel fairly confident that they are real scientists who have proven that scent really is the strongest sense tied to memory.

Surely, I have memories tied to many different scents – my mother's perfume, the roses outside my childhood home, fresh baked bread – but there is only one which moves me to tears every time. My mind can recreate a whisper of it right now. I just closed my eyes to try and make it easier. Losing one sense heightens the others, right?

The damndest thing is that I can't even tell you exactly which memory I'm remembering. It's all of them, I suppose. All of the memories, all at once. Memories from my room, memories from my home, memories from the streets I walked. I see people's faces swimming in my mind, I remember snippets of conversations, stupid mistakes, feelings of joy... all at once.

I'm remembering when I lived in Slovakia for a year. I served as a volunteer and lived with a Slovak family whom I had never met before. Only exchanged a few emails and pictures. After I had been there for a few months, my mother sent me a care package. Over that year, she sent a few care packages, so I can't remember exactly what was in this particular box. Some little teddy bears, a card probably. And a bottle of lotion.

That blessing-of-a-curse bottle of lotion.

It smelled like a dark flower. Not too bright or cheery. A little bit heavy. It seemed to capture my life experience then. Thousands of miles away from my family. Trying to learn a new language. Accidentally stepping on all kinds of cultural landmines.

And this lotion, I only ever used it while I lived in Slovakia, never before then and never since. It's probably a small miracle that it even made it back to Texas, because as I packed up to leave Slovakia, I had to be quite judicious in what I chose to take or leave behind. I left all kinds of clothes, papers, even the teddy bears from my mom. But I took this half-used bottle of lotion, and it has been a portal to my other life ever since.

I can almost smell it right now, even though it is closed and tucked away in my bathroom cabinet. But that faint trace of its scent in my mind is enough to bring back a year's worth of memories. All at once. The good and the painful. It's a wound and a cure all in one blow.

In the ten years since I have returned from Slovakia, I have occasionally opened the lotion and taken a good long whiff, wondering if the scent would still affect me or not. It's almost a game. And every time, the lotion wins. The scent takes me back to a place thousands of miles away and twists my gut and tugs my heart at the same time. I loved my time there, and I miss it, terribly. But it was so hard. My memories are a swirl of incredible people, personal growth, and challenges overcome, mixed with headaches, mistranslations, and cultural stumbles.

One inhale is all it takes.

Shall I play The Game again? The lotion is only 40 feet away. It isn't under lock and key. If opened, will it smell like any old lotion? Or will it awaken every bittersweet memory of my life from ten years ago?

I've just played The Game.

The lotion won. +

Incarnation

by Deb Grant

Tennessee snow happens. Still, it surprised me. I expected a season of snow in my growing up place in New England. But not where the kudzu covers everything while cicadas sing in the noonday heat.

One Tennessee day the snow came in fat flakes and muffled the land. I took a walk out back of the house, beyond the berm that was too steep for the mower, and the uneven underbrush below a stand of trees. Barely a forest, but thick enough to walk beyond sight of the house. Dense enough to pretend I was much deeper away from home than I was. At the back of the property an ingrown stretch of rusted barbed wire marked a long-forgotten property line. It was there I saw the cloven hoof prints in the snow. It must have jumped the fence. The footprints stood out in the dark leaves and mud that lay beneath the snow. They led to a clearing. Not much of one. Just enough space at the base of a pine between the old limbs and the wind. The pattern in the snow formed a bed. It must have spent the night curling its thin legs and thick haunches against the falling

63

cold. After years of seeing rabbits, muskrats, squirrels, raccoons and possums, the idea of a deer sleeping so nearby my own bed was strangely exciting. I'm not a deer hunter. There were more tracks. I couldn't tell if they were made by one or a family. Deer is uniquely singular and plural. I wish I could have seen it or them. The evidence of the hoof prints was enough to stir my belief and my hope.

I would take other walks in other seasons. If I happened to remember, I would look for the deer, but most of the time my thoughts were near-sighted. By spring, I stopped thinking of them at all.

I was sitting wrapped around my coffee cup at the kitchen table spread with the morning paper. Without looking up or afraid, I sensed something big, an arm's length away in the window. Two deer nibbling at the ground as they walked. They lifted their heads and stared at me with those black lashed eyes and flicking ears. I was their only natural predator for miles. The sight of me did not startle them or delay their gentle foraging. I sat there surprised enough to have to tell my body to take another breath. I felt the stretch of my own smile that doesn't happen often enough when I am alone. Those deer were beautiful. Oh, mind you, they were just deer. Not a rare breed, not particularly large. No points to brag about. Just dark caramel coated creatures with ears and feet, noses and eyes. Hungry and busy with being alive. I saw my reflection on them.

Now, you would think by my reaction that I had never seen a deer before. In fact, I had seen them in the wild and in captivity. I had seen them in the zoos, near highways, on the hikes in the mountains. I had gone many places and seen deer. The difference was that day...when I was reading my paper and drinking my coffee and thinking about little else besides myself, the deer came to me. I have left home and seen deer, but this time the deer came home to me. They came into my backyard. The backyard was forever changed. It was never, ever the same again. The backyard was no longer the backyard. It became more than a place I had to mow. It was and would always be where the deer came to me. What great lengths they came. +

Old Shoes

by Travis Meier

These crowded streets I stand upon and muse,
and dream of things that I have yet to see,
of chasing moons and brighter days I sing,
still hope and pray that it is me you'll choose.
With love, my voice, inspired passions prove,
to speak with care, to give you truth, to know,
that in my humble heart desires grow,
that in my mind it is your smile that moves.
Yet doubt creeps by, in shadows, with a grin,
says you can't win, you always play to fail,
and taunts my long of what I've left behind.
I just smile and deny their words the win.
Let bygones pass and lessons mark the trail.
Old shoes I wear, new hope in you I find. +

The Creek Roars

by Travis Meier

The creek roars
swollen with snowmelt
bringing the power
of death
and life
to everything it touches
as it flows down the mountain
into the world below.

The creek roars
like the Spirit roars
throughout our lives
washing away death
bringing new life
taking us from the mountaintops
down into the world
where Christ has called us to follow. +

The Scroll

by Lisa Hoelscher

You treasure quirky little things, right? Well, I have one for you to add to your collection. There is only one in existence, so you can't have it forever. But I will let you borrow its story for a while.

It's a tiny, handmade scroll fashioned with two wooden dowels anchoring a narrow strip of fine paper. You can find it on the left side of a fireplace mantle in Minnesota, and if you ever visit the particular cabin where it is housed, you would be welcome to examine this little scroll. It will fit in the palm of your hand. As you unfurl it, you will notice the words fit the form of an old-fashioned declaration – a long list of "whereases" that conclude with a "therefore."

The scroll really is a delightful thing, but don't let its quirkiness mislead you into thinking it's of minimal importance. That couldn't be farther from the truth. This is not a joke shop toy. The scroll is a holy relic in my family. Crafted about 15 years ago to mark the inaugural family reunion for a new generation. I have advocated for it to be secured in a locked cabinet or a fireproof box to ensure its longevity for future generations, but alas, its home seems to forever be the left side of the mantle. Gathering a fine layer of dust, I'm sure.

My family is a bit sentimental. (But for the love of God, DON'T tell them I told you that! Their eyes would widen, and they would start to back up and wonder where this conversation was going.) Our story is fairly typical: a few generations ago, my ancestors came over on boats. The Scandinavian side settled in North Dakota. The German side settled in Texas. The two branches became fused when the daughter of one side met the son of the other side out in California while working for the war effort. A letter of my grandmother's confirms they met on her first day there.

Fast-forward six decades, and their heirs gathered in a cabin in Minnesota to begin a new tradition without them. In the absence of any grandparents or great aunts and great uncles, it was time to bring together the aunts, uncles, cousins, first cousins once removed, and second cousins. We were a raucous bunch, committed to spending a few days together eating, playing dominoes, singing (yes, singing), looking through old photos and slides, and telling stories. It was the work of re-membering. Bringing together again things that were separated. Inviting past lives to find a place in the present company with the hope that the little ones among us would at least sense the tug of something bigger than themselves and know that they belonged to a larger family tree. They – we – belong to more than just those we could see in the room.

The beauty of our odd, little, handcrafted scroll is that it was pulling double, maybe even triple, duty. At its reading, it embodied a formal opening to our family reunion. The homespun words gave us a laugh and made us catch our breath with deep emotion as we recognized who was present and who was not. And between those two groups, this scroll, that could fit in the palm of your hand, became a bridge, spanning past, present, and future. +

Mammoth Cave

by Deb Grant

With a group of tourists, I followed the guide from the National Park Service into Mammoth Cave in Kentucky. The way was lit by electric fixtures, cleverly hidden behind rocks. Bright enough for safety but subtle enough not to steal the attention from the cave walls. I had no business being in a cave. I had lost my mind. I'm no spelunker. Claustrophobia has kept me out of caves. The only reason I entered this one was the promise of its size. For the most part, Mammoth Cave kept its promise though I will not mention the part of the cave that was a maze of tunnels that required stooping and no fat on one's hips. Oddly enough, that was not the memory of Mammoth that lingered with me longest.

An area of the cave is called Methodist Church. A church had once stood on the land over the caves, but the name was fitting. That space in the cave was larger than most churches. It was huge. The ceiling soaring like a cathedral. The well-placed lights allowed us to feel the grandeur of it even without stained glass windows.

The guide called the group of 30 to form a circle. There was plenty of space for a large circle of humans. She stood in the center with a lantern in her hand. She nodded to a co-worker who turned off all the lights in the cave. When they were all out except the lantern, she asked us all to close our eyes. Open them at the count of three during which time she turned off her lantern. One. Two. Three.

I opened my eyes and saw nothing. Absolutely nothing. It was the deepest darkness, the most complete absence of light I had ever experienced. I blinked several times to be sure my eyes were even open. Not being able to see the hand in front of my face was no cliché. I could not see the friends I traveled to the cave with or the strangers in the group or the guide. Nothing. There was no horizon line on which to fix my sight. My balance started to feel uncertain. My eyes raced in futile circles looking for any source of light. There was none to be found. The darkness lasted less than a minute. It grew into a few seconds of fright and painful insight. I discovered to my awkward embarrassment that I...I, a human, just a little less than divine and greater than the angels...did not glow in the dark. Humans are enlightened after all, but I discovered that was just a metaphor not a physical description.

I did not possess the ability to generate light. In order to see the whole truth, I needed a source of light outside of myself to get the whole picture. I felt all at once silly, naïve, frozen with fear and very much alone.

The guide in the cave struck a single match. The space flooded instantly with that one flame. It didn't take much. We were still standing in an abundance of darkness, but that single light the size of the tip of a finger gave eyes that were able sight. What we saw first were faces in a circle. What the light did was to vanquish our loneliness and restore our community. We could see each other and be seen. +

The Struggle of Mount Carmel

by Travis Meier

Elijah stood on the mountaintop
the prophets of Baal circling
like lions at the kill
The hungry crowds watched
parched tongues
baited breath
waiting

The altars built
the bulls lay ready
stones and wood stacked
ready to reverence the god
who chose to show up

Blood mixed with water
in the trench around Elijah's altar
waiting and longing
for the living God of Sarah and Abraham

I stand in the pulpit
the prophets of Baal are gone
but not absent
though they are nowhere to be seen
in the sanctuary
they wait

in our homes
to come through flickering screens
to whisper their lies
to proclaim their false gospels
to invade our intimate spaces
with their malicious sweetness
because we have invited them in

The hungry crowds look at me
parched tongues
baited breath
waiting

So I'll speak a word
pray for the Spirit of God to move
beyond my brain's ability to form
and my tongue's to convey
hoping
trusting
longing for the Spirit to move
and I question

Because the crowds go home
perhaps full
for a while
satisfied and ready
for action and love

But the false prophets wait

and blue screens light fires
and talking heads whisper sweet nothings
polluting the intimate spaces
because we let them in

And my spirit sinks
and I wonder
and I ponder
and I think

At least Elijah
got to look
the false prophets
in the eye. +

Runner

by Lisa Hoelscher

In the eighth grade, I decided to join the cross-country running team. I have no idea why. I wasn't particularly athletic or fast, but a friend was doing it, so you know, why not?

On the first morning of practice, I quickly found myself at the back of the pack. Halfway through the course, I was moving at barely more than a fast walk. The coaches were on their bikes keeping track of the group, but my fellow runners were well ahead of me. At one point, I was so far behind that a coach rode over to me and said I could take the shortcut back to the gym. How mortifying. But my legs and lungs were screaming, so I did it.

Once back in the gym with everyone else, I was embarrassed and trying not to cry. I could only see one option. I waited until people cleared out, then I went into the coaches' office and let one of them know that I didn't think the cross-country team was for me. I wanted to quit. Coach Hammond said to me, "do you want to quit because you don't like it or because you were last?"

Even though I was hurting, I had enough sense not to roll my eyes and give him a "what do you think?" look. Actually, I'm not sure I said anything at all, and my silence was speech enough. He told me to stick with it a little longer.

I left the office thinking I would just quit the next week. But I didn't. Nor did I quit the week after that. I finished the whole damn, god-awful season. And yes, I finished last pretty much every single freaking time. Ugh. I hated running.

At the end of the season, the coaches gave out awards. They recognized our fastest runners, our most improved runners, and our runners with the most spirit. I was not eligible in any of those categories and clapped politely when my classmates' names were called. Then they announced the final category. The 110% Award. And whose name did they call?

Mine.

I was... shocked. Awards should honor accomplishments. All I did was not quit, and (let's be real) I *wanted* to quit. I *tried* to quit. I just didn't. I had plenty of opportunities and excuses, but I suppose...

Well, I suppose that as the season went on, I found that I rather liked the way the sky changed colors as the sun rose. And I didn't mind the times we ran by the lake. And I was quite pleased with the cool morning breeze.

Good God, did I *like* running? Surely not.

The fact that I don't like running makes my decision to complete a half-marathon nine years later even harder to understand. But as I told myself when I registered for the race, I wasn't doing it for the running. I was doing it for the views.

The official time allotted for a half-marathon is three hours. I finished in two hours and 53 minutes, and I thoroughly enjoyed the scenery. +

Marinate

---

by Deb Grant

I asked a friend what he needed right now.
The world was upside down with grief and tasted like hatred and death. A chunk of it
was sitting on his shoulders that buckled once or twice before. I couldn't give him what he needed then and was pretty sure I couldn't now, but not asking was unkind.

He is stronger than I know. And wiser.

He said he needed a way to be grounded in compassion, mercy, and kindness.
He was waking up his ability to taste the flavor of compassion by reading stories of intense grace from one human to another human, one potent drop of goodness at a time until there was enough in the pot in which to marinate his own soul. Until the bitterness was overwhelmed with a flavor worth sharing by the ladle or the cradle.

One way to change the flavor of a thing that is bitter or needs more lively flavors is to create a marinade.

The spices may need to be ground, broken, smashed, ripped. The sauce needs to be heated, stirred, reduced. A reduction of flavor.

If we were ground up, heated, stirred, and reduced to a sauce, what would we taste like these days?

What could we do to change our bitterness or find our best flavor?

What could we do to be grounded in compassion, mercy and kindness?

We could marinate in a manger.
Not the one whose memory was mutated into mush and refrigerator magnets
But the one who is salty savory sweet and sour.

We could be stirred and ladled or cradled into this world so hungry for the flavor of compassion.
We could be the feast that is so close
we can all taste it
on our fingertips. +

Too Long for Memory to Be Alone

by Travis Meier

Your name is carved in weathered, gray, still stone
A thousand years forgotten on this hill.
The titles faded, your works unfulfilled,
too long for memory to be alone.
Columns collapsed like so many fallen
trees in the shadow of St. Helen's peak
the work to rebuild not counted in weeks
but lifetimes in some pots' scrawling pen.
I'll tell your tales to drifters down the road.
In bars by lights dim and concerts halls full,
your words and deeds with power to pull
the strings of song, the glory you're owed.
Lest we forget the names and lives of old,
that bind the mortar of this weary world. +

Created

by Travis Meier

CREATED
from the dust
of imagination and love
called good.
GIVEN
the breath of life
into expanding flesh
raised into relationship.
ADOPTED
by the divine
heir to the promise
one of eternity.
BELOVED
just as
the changing seasons
and everlasting life. +

Heaven

by Lisa Hoelscher

"Do you not remember who you are?" my friend texted to me, along with a smiley face emoji. She was trying to cheer me up and boost my confidence in a moment of melancholy. (By the way, thank God for friends who think you are a rockstar.)

I was sure that I was not equipped to deal with the challenge in front of me, and I couldn't imagine facing it and coming out unscathed on the other side. I had reached out with a sarcastic word of martyrdom. Her playful response was meant to raise my spirits with a laugh, which I suppose it did in the first moment after I read it. But in the next moment, my eyes watered and my chest tightened.

Had I forgotten who I was? Perhaps I never knew who I was at all. My flippant text message suddenly spawned an existential crisis, something that I absolutely did not have time for. Lest panic overtake me, the Spirit revealed her presence just then.

One moment I was asking the primordial question, "who am I?" and before I could even think the full sentence, the Spirit answered.

"Oh, child. Dear child. We know who you are. You belong to the Enduring Three, the Enduring One. Your life will take different shapes and different hues, but We will always recognize you. How could We not? You belong to Us. Remember who you are."

That's when I learned what heaven is like: it's the place where you never have to wonder if you belong.

My body may have been anchored to the floor by my knees, but my spirit was on the move.

I sensed a transformation. I was shedding a coat which no longer fit and donning something new - a fresh understanding of my place in the world. My confusion gave way to clarity, and I knew, *I knew*, who I was. Who I am.

I am a beloved child of the Enduring Three, the Enduring One. My life will take different shapes and different hues, and through all the changes, I still belong. +

Mug

by Deb Grant

Requiem
My favorite mug broke today.
Rather it flung itself out of the cabinet.

As with any suicide, one wonders
What signals did I miss?
Was there something I could have done?

I loved it enough not to put it in the dishwasher,
but I often loved my coffee more and
wanted more coffee
and the cup was diminutive
compared to the others
that held the vat of caffeine I preferred.
I loved it enough not to put it in the resale shop
box when I moved.
I loved it enough to ask
the keep or pitch question: Does it spark joy?
The answer always saved its life.

It was made by monks in a priory in Vermont. The
monk who made it told me he wanted the glaze to

capture the Vermont dawn...the cool, thick blue-gray haze of a New England morning.

The mug held a piece of the beauty of what I loved about New England without having to remember how I hated scraping my windshield in the winter.

Now that splendid mug will never hold my coffee again. The grief is real. Compared to other griefs it has to be shoved aside. By itself, however, the broken bits still hold the grief as surely as it held my coffee and a memory.

Grief is real. Even the size of a coffee cup.

Redemption

The Japanese art of kintsugi.

It means golden repair.

It is an art form that takes excruciating practice and care, the right tools, and the right training.

I have none of the above. I only dapple at DIY and run from getting any good or even close to getting anything right.

The ancient ones make art.

I wanted to save my mug from the trash.

I made quick work of this mug repair with what I had on hand and what I could learn from a few quick kintsugi videos.

The art form is a spiritual process
of leaning into the brokenness,
allowing the scars to become visible
bold with gold,
finding beauty in our imperfection.

I am one of those people who
leans too well into her brokenness.
I spend too much time in
the land of If Only I Had...
I am not one who boasts except about not
boasting "I've never had a moment of regret!"
I see the broken shards
that my careless words or neglect created.
I see faces of those who walked away angry or
disappointed.
I try not to let it chew up an hour,
because life is short.
But it is still long enough to learn from the scars
and long enough not to boast of much.

I know I haven't paid enough attention.
I haven't lingered in the moment.
I have focused on the past or the future,
but not the now.
I haven't paid attention.
It is why my mug broke.

It is why our world is broken.
At least, my share of it.

The grief is real.
There is no unity possible.
Redemption perhaps.
Golden repair that does not ignore but embraces
imperfection
so that we all might live with the grief.

It will take the rest of our lives
and our children's lives
and their children's lives
if there is a world left.
Time to stop rushing forward or
wallowing in our arrogance or regret.
My mug is now a timepiece.
It measures now in gold. +

'Til Our Hope Becomes a Reality

by Travis Meier

Throughout the ages, all the wars of guns
and steel, find no fuller fields than what lay
before the eyes and tears of all, the ones
who've fallen fast and sudden in these days.
What cannot be seen has taken its toll
across our lands, our terrestrial home,
to leave behind the ones who call the roll,
who stare at empty chairs, themselves alone.
We look to the helpers who work long days
on the front lines to help stop the spread and
break death's pace. Those who discover the ways
to manipulate, and recreate strands,
the building blocks of all our lives to be.
'Til our hope becomes a reality. +

Tattoo

by Lisa Hoelscher

The only tattoos on my body are those put there by God and the sun. Freckles, moles, blemishes, and dark spots. I know some people whose entire life is displayed on their skin. Images inked there are like book chapters telling the story of births, deaths, diagnoses, and triumphs. I am not opposed to other people's tattoos, but I've ruled them out for myself, generally speaking.

Even without tattoos, many new chapters of life have obvious, visible changes or rituals to mark the milestones. Some don't. I recently came upon just such a new chapter when I decided to write more and share my writings with others. It was a big shift for me, and I wanted to mark the occasion. But with what?

Not a tattoo, I groaned. There had to be another option.

A piece of jewelry then? Something that I would wear every day. Something that I would have to choose to put on. I settled on a slender, colorful ring.

At first, I was happy to put it on. But then it didn't fit right. Then I didn't like which finger it was on. Then I didn't like that it brought the total number of rings I wear to three. It quickly became a nuisance, but I kept putting in on. Every day.

After a few months, it still surprises me when I look at it. "Oh yeah," I think. "That's right, I'm a writer now." I trust that others have had the same weird, squishy feeling during a time of transition when a new identity takes root and pushes other things around to make room for itself. It's a bit uncomfortable, a bit unsettling.

But I keep putting on the ring. It has become more than a sign of my writing. It has become a sign that I can trust myself, that I can do something new, that I can heed my inner voice. It will be a permanent fixture on my person.

Geez, it might as well be a tattoo. +

The Lines on Our Palms

by Travis Meier

The lines on our palms
are set
etched in the womb
a sign of identity
a static record
of being created.

The callouses on our hands
allude to reforming
a living skin
growing and working and adapting
through sweat and pain,
joy and tears,
in compassion
through change
for our shared future. +

The Fine Line

by Lisa Hoelscher

The neighborhood of my childhood forms an excellent circuit for pint-sized bike riders. It is a mushed circle with all of the obstacles a kid could want. If you pedal out of my driveway and turn left, you find yourself completing the track clockwise. The first leg is a wide, flat turn which then dumps you into a steep hill. You'll really pick up some speed on that hill. You have to be careful, though, because directly at the bottom is a sharp right turn. I once picked up too much speed and instead of making the turn (which at that pace would have surely sent me skidding off my bike) I was slowed down by rolling into the grassy ditch in front of me.

But let's assume you get to the bottom of the hill at just the right speed and execute the thrilling right turn. Your mind could then relax on the straightaway, but your legs would still need to pump the pedals. After another sharp right turn, you have a little break before you have to give careful attention to your steering. There is an s-shaped curve with a couple of deep divots in the pavement that must either be avoided entirely or accommodated by raising up from your seat so you won't be jostled off. Once past the divots, you're home free.

I knew the course well, and I would often look at the trees or yards as I went by. One day, after I had sailed down the hill, pumped up the straightaway, and turned into the little break, I glanced upwards, and the scene in the sky caused me to slam on the brakes.

It was evening, and the sky was perfectly divided into two distinct colors. The right side was a clear, rich blue, and the left side was a blanket of bright orange clouds. No holes or breaks, just solid orange. Where the colors met, it looked as if someone had taken a curling iron and carefully, gently rolled back the edges of the orange clouds.

After I recovered from the striking sight, I raced home to get my mother's camera. My little legs were working fast. I pounded through the s-shaped curve. I avoided the divots that might slow me down. I slid into the driveway, laying my bike down quickly so that I could fetch the camera with all due haste.

The shortest route back to the spot of the sighting was to reverse my last path. Back around the divots, through the double curve, and then a quick

U-turn so I could look up at the divided sky. It was still divided.

But I was too late. The sun had set lower. The sky on the right was still clear and rich, and while the wall of clouds on the left held their neatly curled shape, the color had shifted to a murky gray.

I was devastated. As I was racing home just a few minutes before, my mind had thought, "what a sight!" I knew that if I could get it on film, I could enter it into my school's art contest, an exciting prospect since I *never* had good ideas for art contests. To this day, I draw human hands the way I did as a child, i.e. like five sausages protruding from a circle. But there in the sky was a piece of art. If I could just capture it. I even had a title ready, "The Fine Line."

It wasn't to be.

The image would be burned in my memory but not on film.

I pedaled home a little slower. But after that, every time my bike took me around the wide, flat turn, down the steep hill, up the straightaway, and around the corner, I would gaze heavenward, wondering if the atmosphere would recreate the picture of a sky split in half, of clouds curled back, of striking contrast between blue and orange. And if it did, I was ready to pedal home for the camera even faster. At least that's what I tell myself. In truth, perhaps I would have just stayed put and watched the clouds change color.

To this day, the work known as "The Fine Line" hangs in the gallery of my mind, a favorite piece in my collection. +

Southern Cross

by Deb Grant

I took a trip on a working ship. The freighter crossed the equator. I've seen the globe with grids of latitude and longitude. I half-expected to see the line of the equator stretching from port to starboard as we crossed over it. Days passed when I didn't see another ship. Even a tiny silhouette on the horizon. From Northern hemisphere to the Southern, the night sky slowly filled with stars I had never met. I stopped looking for the Big Dipper and started looking for the Southern Cross.

It was my father who helped me find the Big Dipper. Find the North Star bright and then look left or right depending on the time of night. I was taking the trip my father would have taken had he lived. I had to be my own stargazer, constellation finder. The quest for the Southern Cross began in earnest with the equator crossed. Four stars in the pattern of a cross with the right-hand star just slightly higher than the left. There were so many, and I was easily confused. There was no one who could point. No long arm and tenderness I could use for a telescope to follow to his fingertips.

I sat on the open deck above the bridge. It was like being on a roof of a many storied building in the middle of the ocean. I was only a passenger who paid for the ride. I was not a bridge officer trained to steer a ship with a sextant and their wits if the ship's guidance systems lost power. I didn't know where to start looking. I couldn't speak the language of the sky.

Night after night I looked and failed. I gave up my pride and asked a member of crew to help me find it. He looked and pointed to the sky and said, "There." and I said, "There?" and he said, "There!" and after a few more rounds, I decided I had taken too much of his time and so I lied. I said, "I see it now! Thank you so much!"

One night I was sleeping in my cabin and gently woke as if someone whispered my name. I didn't move my head from my pillow or open my eyes right away. I felt the constant movement of the ship. The thrum of the engine. The pitch and roll. When I opened my eyes, I looked up at the night sky through the cabin window just above my bed. The stars framed within the windowpane moved side to side, out of frame then back again. And there, right there, framed in my little window as if it were waving to me, over and over again...was the Southern Cross. It waved as if the stars were balancing on the tips of fingers of an outstretched hand. It was as if I did not find it, but it found me. This constellation that ancient mariners used to find their way home waved to me and sent me on my way. +

ABOUT THE AUTHORS

Deb Grant is a human living under the laws of gravity in Houston, Texas. Grant is the author of 7 previous books, Pedestrian Theology, ELOGOS Daily Devotions for Down to Earth Disciples 1, 2, & 3, Passage: Lenten Devotions, and two books of poetry: Storm and Nuevo Vino.

A native of New England, Grant earned her undergraduate degree from Barrington College (now Gordon College). She earned a Master of Divinity from Trinity Lutheran Seminary, Columbus, Ohio. Grant was ordained in 1981, serving as a pastor in the Evangelical Lutheran Church in America in Goodlettsville, Tennessee; Clemson, South Carolina; College Station, Texas and Dickinson, Texas. After 37 years in parish and campus ministry, Grant retired. She continues to write, create art pieces, care for her friends and use her art and words whenever possible for the greater good. Most of the time she is the humble servant to her dog and bird.

Deb Grant's Contact Information:
Email: revdeb@jazzwater.com
Websites: jazzwater.com
　　　　　　debgrant.substack.com
Etsy Shop: www.etsy.com/shop/Jazzwater
Facebook: facebook.com/Elogosbydebgrant

Lisa M. Hoelscher is desperately trying to be a morning person but to no avail. She blames her lack of success on staying up too late coupled with ushering two young children out the door every morning. Though her beloved husband is nearing sainthood, even he cannot pull his wife towards a better regimen.

Hoelscher earned a bachelor's degree in political science and English literature from Texas A&M University and then served for one year in Slovakia as a Young Adult in Global Mission. Back in the States, she completed her Master of Divinity from Luther Seminary in St. Paul, Minnesota, and soon after her ordination in December 2019, the whole world changed. She is committed to shaping the Church's response.

She currently lives in San Antonio, Texas and serves as a pastor in the Evangelical Lutheran Church in America. She can be reached via her website at www.thoughtsandwonderings.com.

ABOUT THE AUTHORS

Travis Meier is a poet, a picker, and a pastor. You'll often find him, cup of coffee in hand, nose in a book on theology or history, with half his mind on the past and the other wrestling with reconciling the present to God's unfolding kingdom.

Meier earned his undergraduate degree in English literature from Texas A&M University and a Master of Divinity from the Lutheran School of Theology in Chicago in Chicago, Illinois. He was ordained in 2013 and has served churches in Fredericksburg, Texas and College Station, Texas.

He currently lives in College Station with his wife Kristen, who specializes in all things glitter and art. They work together making sure the world has enough roses and a place for all at the table. Their house is run by two dogs who are the best at all things, but mostly naps. Contact Travis through his blog: thebartimaeuseffect.substack.com.

To purchase more copies of Beacon Hunters:

- Jazzwater.com
- Order from local independent book store
- Amazon.com

Other publications by Deb Grant:
The Jesse Tree
Pedestrian Theology
ELOGOS Daily Devotions for Down to Earth
        Disciples. Volumes 1, 2, & 3.
Passage: Lenten Devotions
Storm
Nuevo Vino

Available at Jazzwater.com or Amazon.com

CPSIA information can be obtained
at www.ICGtesting.com
Printed in the USA
LVHW022038070621
689597LV00017B/2364